All Scripture references taken from the KJV of the Holy Bible, unless otherwise indicated.

Church *Craft: Witchcraft in the Church*

by Dr. Marlene Miles

Freshwater Press 2024

freshwaterpress9@gmail.com

ISBN: 978-1-963164-68-8

Paperback Version

Table of Contents

Church *Craft*

Freshwater Press, USA

Church *Craft*

Some folks don't tolerate lies well; I am one of those folks. No, I'm not perfect, but I seek to be honest and not lie *every* day.

I am also one of those people who look for the *motive* behind why a person did a thing or said a thing. I have been mocked by that, but we are all wired and gifted by God the way that we are. I look for why I, myself am motivated to do or say a thing; I am not just looking at other folks. I suppose we all should do that to be as honest with ourselves as possible. This will help us grow spiritually, mentally, and emotionally.

I have had the unfortunate experience of having gone to many churches over the years and like my experience with going to Best Buy, which I've shared before, going into that store or into a church **with a husband,** (or a man, any man) is far different than going in alone, or as a single.

Best Buy salespeople, who can be any type, from young novices to more experienced computer geeks have always ignored me when I come into the store alone, as if I wandered in thinking it was a grocery store or something. There is no respect given to the fact that I know where I am, came there on purpose, know what I want, and came to buy. I should be a salesperson's dream, but I am ignored.

Also, I know why I go to church. I know what a church is, why it is there, and why I came there in the first place. Most often it is because **God sent me.** Before attending or even joining a church, I have prayed about what church to attend. On some occasions it has been because it is logically a good church that is teaching what I want to learn or is offering something that I need such as prayers of a certain type, or worship at a certain level.

Sometimes it has been by location, which is not the best reason to choose to go to a particular church, but if that is the best church for a person to attend logistically, sometimes you may go to your closest church. On the other hand, the church you attend may be far away, but God may be *sending* you there. In the same way, sometimes the church that an evangelist may speak at is far away, but God *sends* them there. This should be the reason why popular preachers may travel so much--- God *sends* them to where they should be preaching next.

Perhaps. Yet we know that sometimes people send themselves, or worse, the devil sends folks places too.

But, because of the experiences of being treated differently when going to a church as a single versus as a married person, I pity the singles. Seriously, not to create a party club, but somebody ought to just start a church for singles so the married people, who should be converted, and are not, won't ostracize, criticize, or reject them for no good or Godly reason at all. In this singles church, everyone will start out accepted and on the same footing.

Possibly.

Sure, family is the backbone of society, but the way singles are treated in churches is a crying shame from my experiences. They are treated differently and not in a good way. They are treated differently, and this ought not to be so.

For there is no respect of persons with God.
(Romans 2:11)

In this alleged singles church, once singles meet and marry, what then? I don't know, I haven't thought about it that much, but I think they could all stay there together unless the unmarried singles there are unconverted and resort to worldly tactics to get a spouse, especially the women. And unless the men feel it is a Christian nightclub and try to date all the single ladies in the place. Of course, if there is conversion, if people fully put on Christ, they won't misbehave in any of these ways.

What am I saying? If the married and insecure folks fully put on Christ, there would have been no need to start a singles church in the first place.

Conversion can take a while, *huh*?

Well, after saying all that, I realize that whoever pastors a place like this has to be a real pastor and not a wolf guarding the sheep, him or herself.

Neither getting saved, nor joining a church affords anyone the opportunity to do whatever they please. Mixing this with that, especially spiritually is not indicated, nor is it cool--, no matter who is running this thing.

Female singles being rejected and treated poorly is the first example of Church *Craft* that I have ever encountered in any church, yet it has happened in nearly every church I've ever attended where I did not have a spouse. I have never been rejected with a spouse, mostly because the church loved the spouse and wanted him, versus me. However, in my marriage(s), in my case, I was almost always the breadwinner or the top financial giver, but being married it looked as though the man was. I was the one insisting that we tithe at whatever church we belonged to but that man was still celebrated like every Sunday was his birthday or something. Were these churches after the male, the money, or both?

For some months, I went to a new church that required 24 weeks of New Members Class before anyone could join any ministry in that church. About 4 or 5 weeks into that class, a young man asked me out for coffee after church. He chose Panera. The only problem is when I got there, he said he was parked in the back and I should come park near him. I thought that was weird, but the parking lot was kind of full, so I did. This man wanted to make a pass at me in the back of the coffee shop, and he had no intentions of going into Panera and buying me a coffee or sharing any type of conversation.

Does this sound weird to you?

Oh, that's not the weird part of this story, the following week, Week 6 into the mandatory 24-week New Members class this guy was on the stage playing the drums with the Praise Team.

Now, tell me what you think.

Church *Craft* boils down to playing up to the one they want, and disdaining the one they do not feel is important.

But if ye have respect to persons, ye commit sin, and are convicted of the law as transgressors. For whosoever shall keep the whole law, and yet offend in one point, he is guilty of all. (James 2:9-10)

Am I saying that discrimination in the church is a thing? Yes, I am. This is not about color, most often it is about gender--, yes, even in a *professed* church. Sometimes it is by anointing, which we will get into later. But discrimination, being a "respecter of persons" is witchcraft, plain and simple. When it happens in the world, aren't we so quick to call it out?

It's witchcraft?

Yes.

When it happens in a church, what is it called? Church *Craft*, a phrase that describes witchcraft in the church, and it's not pretty.

10

Do these women, do these people realize that they are doing this to single females? Single females are being treated as if they are in a math class and even though they are making A's, they are being treated worse than the male who is making C's and D's because he is a male.

As a single, I visited a church with a man I was dating. I went to one adult Sunday School class, he went to another, so the elder-instructor didn't know I was with someone. This teacher happened to be teaching on the Book of Acts, and I happened to be studying the Book of Acts on my own all that previous week. He began asking his class some questions from last week's teaching and they all sat looking at him like a box of rocks. So, after a few long silences where no one knew or was confident enough to answer the teacher's question, I raised my hand and answered. After I answered the third question the teacher told me in these words, *"You need to shut up and let someone else answer."*

He didn't realize that no one else knew an answer or was responding.

Some months later, the man I went to that church with was asked to be an elder. In the car, leaving the parking lot, he asked me what is an elder? He also confided that the Pastor had told him that he would find something for him to do because he was a good giver. This man's mother was a pastor in his hometown, and he resented her and knew nothing of spiritual things, God, the Bible or prayer.

What is an elder? Yeah, he really asked me that. I'll tell you what it's not. It is not someone who knows nothing of spiritual things, God, the Bible, prayer or someone who tells people who know how to answer Bible questions to shut up.

The fellow I was dating also asked me, What is Azuza? Yet this is the one that was being promoted in a ministry and I was the one told to shut up. When this fellow would pray over food for example, vegetable soup, he would say thank you for each vegetable--- by name, carrot, potato, tomato, peas… that was his idea of prayer. I thought he was joking when he first did this, because it took so long that the soup got cold, but he was not joking; this was his level.

What is an elder, and what is not an elder?

Lord, help us all; that's the one that particular pastor wanted to promote into a highly spiritual office.

So, the single female continues to look for a church home as they call it. And, also for a suitable husband, because this one is not fully formed but being promoted within an *organization* with a 501C. You cannot buy your way into the Kingdom of God, but perhaps you can get a position in a "church" with money.

The reason a single woman may have come to the church is because the world is treating her poorly. Only to come to a church and bear open her soul for the church to treat her the same, or worse. That is a shame before God.

My God of Mercy! Is there any sanctuary? And, where might that sanctuary, that safe haven be?

Until I went into the sanctuary of God,
(Psalm 73:1A)

The point is, if the sanctuary (Exodus 25:8) is where God dwells and meets up with man, then where God is there should also be peace for whomever is in that place.

Really? When is that going to start?

Do these people know that they are being evil to others?

I don't know, that's for God to say. But most grown people know what they are doing and their own <u>motivation</u> for doing that thing. So, they probably are aware that they are doing it, even if it is laying up stones of offence against the unsuspecting folks who come into a place expecting to find the Love of God.

Do You Want My Man?

The insecurity of women is glaring, both in the streets and in the church. You can tell by how many social media beefs there are between women, over a man. So these insecurities are not about not having enough money, or enough food--, no it is about not having the emotional support, attention, and loyalty that they may want or need in interpersonal relationships, specifically, marriage.

Relationships can be *suspect* even of couples in the church, but that is only told by how either of a "couple" behaves when around others. Men, what are you doing to make your wife feel secure? Anything? Nothing? Do you know if your wife feels secure in your relationship or not? Then no wonder the single female who comes through the church doors gets the side-eye from the married women, older or not, who may be sitting in the pew silently asking the question, *Do you want my man?*

I went to a wedding as a plus one; I didn't know any of the people there except my date. I kid you not, when the bride stood at the double doors from the foyer to begin her wedding procession to the altar, her eyes caught mine. I thought she was beautiful and probably smiled at her. She rolled her eyes at me. She ruined *her* entire wedding **for me**. I could have had such a nice time, but it was horrible.

I don't even know these people and live several states away. I couldn't figure it out, until finally, perhaps, maybe, I looked like someone who her husband-to-be knew or had cheated on her with? Perhaps I looked like someone she had previously hated, or still hated?

I promise you I do not know what that was about, but women often have looked at me as if I have something that belongs to them.

I do not. I have what belongs to me, what God gave to me, and I intend to keep what the Lord has entrusted to my hands and to my life.

Anyhoo---,

Ask yourself, do you even want your own man?

Do you want a man that you can't trust because you think if he *sees* a female, even in a church, or says hello to a female that means they are going to strike up a relationship? Do you think the presence of a single woman in a building is too much pressure for your husband to stand up under? Do you even have a marriage if that is a problem or a concern in your relationship, or in your mind? Is your husband saved? Are you? Are either or both of you converted to the image of Christ yet? Why is this kind of stuff happening in a church?

And, if your husband has the roving eye, why must it be the woman's fault? If you plan to control every woman your husband comes into contact with, you've got a real problem. Men are often the pursuers in connections, but if you've got a lustful, greedy husband, he needs deliverance. If your husband is <u>your</u> husband and you two have a proper relationship, then how is that single woman who just came in the doors, in any state she may be in, dressed up, disheveled, all put together, needing deliverance, not needing deliverance --, ready to teach and preach, with no children, or with 5 children trailing behind her--, why is *she* the problem, and not your husband?

How is she the problem when he's done this before, or more than once before? You know before he ever met her or laid eyes on her. Stop yourselves from doing this or get deliverance. How is *she* the problem? Why must she be rejected or not receive ministry because of the evil in your own heart?

> Unto the pure all things are pure: but unto them that are defiled and unbelieving is nothing pure; but even their mind and conscience is defiled. (Titus 1:15)

How is she the problem and not you, yourself, or you and your husband for not developing a proper relationship this past 4 years, or 10 years or ever how long you two have been married?

Unlike Best Buy when the single female comes in the sales reps think she doesn't want anything. **At church when the single female comes in the older married women think that she wants <u>everything.</u>**

Even sadder, they think she can get it and they are worried that she wants *their* man--, because he's the best male in the place? Or, is he the lowest woman chaser in the place? But they treat this woman as though she will steal their man, and they will be somehow diminished or left out in the cold.

Honestly, Reader, I'll tell you that I've met very few women who want me anywhere around their man. I do not want their men. I do not flirt with their men. I do not come on to their men. I do not dress or talk seductively. I do nothing to entice anybody's anybody, yet women do not want me around their man. EVEN IN A CHURCH.

Of course, every male pastor I've ever tried to sit under, except two of them has hit on me. I promise you; it has gotten so old. I'm not putting anything out there to catch anyone's man, especially not a married man, and especially never a pastor. It is often, why I leave churches. Yes, I have a good talk with God, but when the pastor is hitting on you, you cannot receive spiritually from that person. Worse, if the pastor is behaving that way, then all the men are under that grace, or in this case, that disgrace, unless they are very strong in the Lord on their own.

Please have Wisdom enough to know that if he's doing it to you, you are not the only one. Not by a long stretch of the imagination.

So current ladies of the congregation, perhaps you should worry. Current ladies, you should worry if your first lady is worried about what her husband is doing because eventually it will all trickle down from the head. It always does.

But, this is no reason to blame the single woman who just came into the church.

I knew such a man whose eyes roved creepily up and down every woman he saw. We were supposed to be in a relationship. Oddly, I never got jealous that he did it wondering what *she* had that I didn't. Instead, I saw him as a predator and felt sorry for the women he did this to. I got out of that connection as soon as I realized that he was not seeing what he was doing and no one in the church we attended bothered to tell him or help him be delivered of this. It was **him**, not the women that he groped with his eyes.

Does anybody trust anybody with anybody these days? *Even* in the church?

Mistreating a single woman is *extra* sad because God may have just sent in another worker to the fields that are white to harvest. God could have sent in a spiritual gift that will help this ministry and this church. God may have sent in extra tithes and offerings to bless the people that church is supposed to bless.

Many have entertained or disdained angels, unaware.

Very sad, because the church is predominantly women, these days. But instead, too many see a single woman as a threat. And that's another opening for Church *Craft*, and the unconverted souls fall for it and begin their strategy against this single female. They start the foul polygamous-like witchcraft, the foulest of all witchcraft, in my opinion. It incorporates hatred, reproach, rejection and condemnation and all those actions are evil. The shortsightedness here is that if the coveted male doesn't choose the new single female, it doesn't mean that he will choose you, especially if he hasn't chosen you before he saw (if he even saw) the new female. There are billions of other people in this world. Are you planning to oppose and attack each one until he chooses you?

Polygamous witchcraft: when this is happening in the church, it is Church *Craft*.

When they choose the male and shun the female this is favoritism, and it is supported by witchcraft as well.

But if ye have **respect** to **persons**, ye commit sin, and are convicted by the law as transgressors. (James 2:9)

If God says that the people who are saved are accepted in the Beloved, then perhaps those who do not accept God's people are not *of* the Beloved. They say favor is not fair, but favoring one somebody doesn't mean that you disdain or disrespect another. Favoritism anywhere --, in a family, in a church, or at work will cause jealousy, resentment, and hurt feelings. Without Christ the one being disrespected may resort to evil and witchcraft themselves.

Those who do are playing with God, deceiving themselves, they are evil and not representing God.

Not only that, there is judgment associated with such disobedience, hatred and misbehavior. Didn't Jonah reject the people of Ninevah? Look what happened to him. That female coming through the church doors that fateful Sunday when she decided she needed spiritual help could be named Ninevah. She could be *from* Ninevah. God could have sent her there for help, but instead she got hurt— church hurt by Church *Craft*, stealthily trying to hide in the pews, or in some cases, in the pulpit.

Jonah was not just a pew member sent to Ninevah, he was a preacher, a prophet of the pulpit variety. He was all the more accountable for his detestable behavior regarding where God *sent* him.

If this single, supposed vixen could get any man she wants, why would she want *your* man? And if she did, wouldn't she already have him? And if she was such a *femme fatale*, wouldn't she already have a man? Didn't she come to church for spiritual reasons, not to date or get a husband? Didn't you come to church with a pure heart? Why do you think she didn't? *Haters*, think this through, please. Whether it is fear, or whether you have idolized your man, everybody doesn't want your husband.

To the pure, all things are pure.

BTW, discriminating against people, being a respecter of persons, treating people who come into your establishment very poorly is not profitable at all: Best Buy is closing stores.

Seducing Spirit

In the average church, everyone seems to want the pastor's attention and favor; an egotistical pastor likes it like that, it makes him feel big and important. However, it is his responsibility, when possible, to build people up and that takes attention and interaction. He must be careful not to overdo it and not to carry a *seducing spirit* that draws people in the wrong way.

For example, I've met men in the world who carry that kind of *spirit* where they make you feel that you are the only person in the world, when you're with them. I am calling that a *seducing spirit*—not so much that the person wants to draw you into error – well, they kinda do, because they are trying to draw you into worshipping them, making themselves your favorite--, making themselves a human altar.

Trust that they want you to feel as though you are the only other person in the world when you are with them, but, **only** when you are with them. They treat everyone this way. When they are not in your company, you can't find them, not by cell, not by text. You cannot find them. (That's a clue.)

Much like the guy with the crawling eyes, a woman may first reject that creepy attention, but then she may buy into it believing he is really into her. He's not. He's a creepy guy who does this to every woman. The guy who love bombs you is also using witchcraft and this should not be in the church. If he is innocently doing it then he is co-dependent and needs deliverance. I'm saying, you are totally wonderful, I'm sure you are--, but watch out for *seducing spirits.*

That's a *spirit*, and it is not of God. Yeah, there is a phenomenon of women falling into like or love or lust or something with the pastor. In this case both the lady and the pastor are practicing Church *Craft.* We pray the pastor is not over-*nicing*, or over smiling or whatever to get the parishioner to volunteer for some church work.

Everyone wants to be noticed. Everyone wants the most anointing. Everyone wants the microphone and to be part of the "show." Everyone wants to be seen and be special. Those who don't mind lying, acting and pretending will give you the attention you are craving to get what they want from you. It may not be real. It may not last, but that's what love bombing is. It is also witchcraft or Church *Craft* if it is done in a "church."

If someone has father issues and needs a father's love; this is very telling. It is telling that they have never had it or had it genuinely. Pastor or not, when a man is not giving his wife and family at home what they should be getting at home, that truth will spill out in public--, even in a church. If she is prideful, or still cares in the least, that woman will try to be controlling and try to make it look as though their relationship is fine, even though it may not be. This is also Church *Craft*—it is **manipulation**. She is the one who secretly is most worried as to what her husband will do because of a new single female in the church.

Needing love, real, *agape* love is the plight of society, and unconverted souls who never had it, or had it sufficiently cannot bear the thought of someone else getting it, when they, themselves aren't. Specifically, they can't stand the thought of someone else getting it from the person they think they should be getting it from, but they are not.

Years ago, a girlfriend of mine would call me when she got home from work, and we'd chat and chat. Often, I would notice her 8-year-old daughter would be trying to get her attention, as children are known to do especially if you are on the phone. But this friend called me pretty much every day and we'd stay on the phone for hours. This little girl needed her mother. One day when I had had enough, I asked my friend, *What time does your daughter go to bed?*

She said, *Eight-thirty.*

I told her, *"Your daughter needs you. There's dinner, homework and mommy and me time. Please don't call me any evening before 8:30 after your daughter has had her fill of you and is in bed asleep."* Parents, it is your child's prerogative to get so much love from their parents that one day they wake up and realize they don't need you anymore as is the behavior of some rebellious teens.

I told her, *"There may come a time when your daughter doesn't want to have much or anything to do with you. Until that time, give her so much love and attention that she gets filled up or fed up with you."*

Great advice, I thought. But this broke our friendship, because I don't have kids, so how can I dare give her advice, she said.

Oh well, lost a friend? Good for the kid, even if it was bad for me.

Parental, *agape*, Godly love, we all need it and the sooner we get it, starting at birth, the better we develop emotionally and spiritually. If we don't get it during formative years, it is very telling later in life. That husband that I spoke of may be ministering properly to his wife, family, and home. It could be that the wife needs JESUS and deliverance so the voids of not being loved in childhood can be met. Could be the husband doesn't know how to do that, or he is exhausted, or most likely HE IS NOT JESUS and knows it, but maybe wifey doesn't yet know it.

A woman told me that she spent the first five years of her marriage to her husband wondering why he wasn't *making her happy*.

It finally dawned on her that that was not his job. I agreed with her, unless he's a professional clown or something.

But, does this church of which I speak even *have* the Father's Love, *agape* love? In the Book of the Revelation the Church of Ephesus had lost its love without even realizing it.

If you have lost your love for God, as a church or even as an individual, you will treat people like crap. So, I can ask is agape love channeling through the people in that church to others there? Will it channel to others who come through the door who need one-another ministry?

Well, it won't if people are glaring at each other, fake smiling and fake hugging each other because someone with a microphone told them to turn to your neighbor and give them a hug. So, you close your eyes and wrinkle somebody's suit and knock their pretty church hat off their head. What good did any of this do?

So, hug someone? No don't, and let's not say we did. Hugs are so fake. It would be better to look your church neighbor in the eye and ask him or her, "How are you? How are you, *really*?"

Fake hugs, fake friends, and fake church members to me are like: They say they are for peace, but really, they are for war, so please don't fake-hug me.

Conversion may take a while, *huh*?

The Non-Relationship

One of the saddest things I've ever seen or experienced: the non-relationship. It is when a couple is together physically, or on paper – they are married, but they are really not in a relationship. It could be that each of them is in a different relationship, or only, **one** of them is in a relationship, but the other is not.

A woman constantly told her brother that she was divorcing her husband. When she visited her brother several times a year the husband called her every night to check on her and see how she was doing. Finally, someone had to ask, and you know it was me, does her husband know that your sister is divorcing him, because he seems very attentive and loving to her? Each of them was in different relationships within the same relationship.

If not married, usually, it is the woman who believes they are in a relationship, or she wants to *will* them to be a couple or wants to present in public as if they are *together*.

It's not totally her fault, because if they had sex prematurely--, and before marriage it is premature sex, then they established an evil covenant with a soul tie. *Goes into* equals married; she believes they are at least a *couple* if not married, or *pre*-married. They aren't necessarily engaged, maybe they are *pre*-engaged in her mind, so they are a couple. Simple—to her.

Even simpler to the guy, they just had sex.

Having sex, to a guy who puts no value on his body or what his body is doing, or ascribing anything spiritual to something that is so spiritual, is just having sex. He doesn't think that anything happened, other than what he saw happen in the bedroom. He is so wrong.

So the woman is now in a relationship and the guy just exercised. He rode his bike 5 or 10 miles, takes a shower and snaps back to who he was and what he was doing before he rode his bike. To the woman, they are practically engaged; they had sex. Yeah, they had sex: she is a bicycle to him. He rode his bike and put it back up in his garage.

It's hardly different than the man driving her really nice car to an event, so they arrive looking appropriate by either or both of their standards, but it is her car. She paid for the tickets to the gala, bought everything they both are wearing but he's holding the tickets so he can appear as the "man." She invested in their relationship.

He doesn't see it that way, he only went to a party.

Well, it goes further, if he is the man, then he's **her** man, she believes she's doing the opposite of emasculating him; she thinks she is building him up and "*masculating*" him which is really not anything that is possible and is probably not even a word. It's only feeding the image-driven life.

This outing, this event is all about **her** which means he cannot look at, see, or talk to another female the entire time they are there. If so, there will be heck to pay. This is domination and control; it is witchcraft. Yeah, this happens out in the world, and also in churches, folks.

She may or may not tell him this, but it is implied. But this man may have no idea that this is the plan or that this is how this works.

Anyhow, all of that is backstory.

Even if she didn't pay for anything, the couple that is not a couple and have no real relationship cannot fake it in public, even at church to make everyone at church *think* they are a couple who are together, satisfying each other's *couple* needs, as a couple should.

Most often she is afraid that someone else will get what she wants or feels she deserves from her husband, or whomever this person is supposed to be to her. And, she's afraid that it will be very obvious that he doesn't really care about her, or that they are not a *couple*, and that she will be humiliated, because this is not a real relationship and other people will start to see that.

I said all that to say that that happens even in churches and that is what makes the polygamous-like witchcraft, glaring looks, side-eyes and hatred prevail, even in a place where God is supposed to be. The woman who is with that man or supposed to be with *that* man, is not really with him, but she wants to *appear* as if she is.

This is on the level of Peninnah giving her co-wife, Hannah grief in their relationship with Elkanah, *their* husband. It's polygamous witchcraft. It's akin to how Leah treated her real-life sister and co-wife to Jacob, their husband because Leah had children by Jacob, but Rachel at that time did not. It's like shouting, *He's mine, he's my husband because of this that or the other*, but the man is not saying anything.

Maybe that's what these women are thinking, *if I have to share my husband with my sister,* even a sister in the "faith."… What a horrendous thought!

Folks, until the man in the relationships <u>says</u> something there is no reason the women should be fighting one another. If he's never going to say who he's with and make a statement as to who is his wife and who is not, then you're dealing with a Shyster. If, by his actions, he never indicates that he's with his wife and not with the person that is not his wife, there will never be peace, even if the women go to rolling eyes, shooting soulish prayers out into the atmosphere or pick up knives for a knife fight.

If that man is not claiming one woman as his wife, then he may not be claiming to even have a wife, so you may as well look out into the world to see if he's looking for another. If he's not claiming one of you, his ego may be fed by both of you making fools of yourselves. If he's not claiming his wife, he's a fraud and a trickster. Is that the man you want?

If he's not claiming you as his wife, then why would you play house with him, pretending to be his wife? In your time of make-believe with this fellow, this new female, who may never notice your fellow, is seen as a threat to the woman who is trying to **MAKE** a relationship happen. Anything and anyone is a threat to a fake relationship, but the new female who comes into the church unescorted is treated as the latest threat as if she is a CAT 5 hurricane.

It can happen that way in a so-called church because God is not there, even though He is supposed to be, or it has been alleged that He is there. Oh, I can't blame the whole church, can I? It can happen that way in the heart of a so-called saved person because God is not in their heart or on the throne of their heart, even though He is supposed to be and they profess that He is there.

Conversion can take a while, sometimes.

What you say with your mouth is very important, and as important or more so is that with the heart God is allowed or disallowed in a person, in a person's soul, especially if that person is priesting over an entire altar.

An *altar*?

Yes.

As soon as a place is declared a "church" and people come there, worship there, give offerings there, and it is declared that the physical interfaces with the spiritual realm there, that is an altar. That is far different than something or someplace that is not declared as a "church." And, it is far more dangerous. So really, it depends on who, and in what position and what authority is that person who is giving the side eye to anyone. If it is someone in the pew that's one thing, and it's bad enough. But when it's coming from a higher position, such as an Elder or someone who priests at the altar of that church, that's another whole thing.

The Gifts & The Gifted

Speaking of the Father's attention, when one soul has any of the spiritual gifts that God, through the Holy Spirit, gives His people, and another is jealous of it--, Lord have Mercy on us all. The spiritually insecure may think that the new female is coming to take their church position away from them.

This could be a reflection of issues in leadership, but it could also be that *conversion* is slow in some and even slower in others, so their worldly attitudes and the evil *spirits* in their souls are on display, even in a church. It could be that the person in that coveted position is not even supposed to be there, and they know it, but they hope no one else does, and they can just remain in that position. A converted soul will celebrate even a newcomer who has the same spiritual giftedness and see it as help from God.

Issues in leadership?

Why yes. As in a family the parents are the leaders. When a family is not getting along, especially because of jealousy, we first look at the leadership of that family or group. Next, we look at the individuals to see what their malfunctions may be.

Mom, Dad, how come you always let brother do so and so, but not me?

Because you're 5 and your brother is 10.

Dad, Mom, how come you let baby Sister sleep in the bed with you when she's scared, but I don't get to?

Because she's a baby and you're not. We treated you the same way when you were a baby, but you don't remember it.

Pastor, how come you let Sister Sally sing a solo on Sundays, but I don't get to?

Because Sister Sally can sing, and your gifting lies elsewhere. So, if you could agree to sing so low that no one can hear you, then sing so LOW...

Pastor, how come you mention Brother So and So's name all the time, but you don't mention mine?

Because you don't do anything in the church and Brother So and So is cleaning up and doing all kinds of support ministries around here.

These kinds of questions and the attitudes and the emotions that they evoke come from people who do not know their identity, purpose, or gifting in the Kingdom of God. It's kind of like Joseph and his brothers who resented Joseph's dreams and his anointing. They lost sight of the fact that they were also stars in the eyes of God. Those jealous brothers were so focused on Joseph's anointing that they lost sight of the fact that they had anointings of their own.

This is not little league or T-Ball where everyone gets the same trophy whether they are athletic or not. Which, by the way, I think is very unfair. Does everyone get an A in Math or Spelling whether they can *math* or spell? Of course not. So, the kid who is smart in the books gets an A in spelling and also a trophy for **not** being athletic, but simply because he is on the T-Ball field.

The kid who is athletic gets the same thing the lack luster player gets and only gets a C in Math, not a trophy--, not an A. The message to that kid from Little League on is, *you are nothing special. Your* A-*level play on the field is not important.* Even though you are in class, you get nothing for that.

But that athletic kid *is* special, we are all special in our own way. We are special in whatever way God says we are. We do not all have the same gifts, talents, and abilities, and we don't disdain the giftings of others. People of God, if we were all the same, God could have just made **one** person and He could have been done with it right then. God could have said*, "There, I made one person. The rest of them will be identical, so no need to make another one."*

We know that God didn't do that.

All the gifts are given by the Holy Spirit. The gifts are named the same, but in individuals, the administration of the gifts are different.

The five-fold ministry gifts:

And He Himself gave some *to be* apostles, some prophets, some evangelists, and some pastors and teachers, for the equipping of the saints for the work of ministry, for the edifying of the body of Christ, till we all come to the unity of the faith and of the knowledge of the Son of God, to a perfect man, to the measure of the stature of the fullness of Christ; that we should no longer be children, tossed to and fro and carried about with every wind of doctrine, by the trickery of men, in the cunning craftiness of deceitful plotting, but, speaking the truth in love, may grow up in all things into Him who is the head—Christ. (Ephesians 4:11-13)

And there are other spiritual gifts.

There are different kinds of spiritual gifts, but the same Spirit is the source of them all. There are different kinds of service, but we serve the same Lord. God works in different ways, but it is the same God who does the work in all of us.

A spiritual gift is given to each of us so we can help each other. To one person the Spirit gives the ability to give wise advice]; to another the same Spirit gives a message of special knowledge. The same Spirit gives great faith to another, and to someone else the one Spirit gives the gift of healing. He gives one person the power to perform miracles, and another the ability to prophesy. He gives someone else the ability to discern whether a message is from the Spirit of God or from another spirit. Still another person is given the ability to speak in unknown languages while another is given the ability to interpret what is being said. It is the one and only Spirit who distributes all these gifts. He alone decides which gift each person should have.
(1 Corinthians 12:4-11 NLT)

God wants us very well endowed with gifts: Prophecy, hospitality, exhortation, mercy, teaching, leadership are other Gifts of the Spirit.

God likes unique, so He does not expect us to copy one another. The Word says to covet the best gifts, but we don't covet people or things. Like a field of flowers, even sunflowers, tulips, cosmos or whatever, they are the same variety, but each one is different from the other; God expects a different expression of the giftings among us. It's one of the reasons God made more than one person.

Still, there are those who copy others. They copy, or try to copy their ministry. They try to copy their revelations, they try to copy another's style. Please know that the Gifts of the Spirit work by Love, so if you don't have love, you ain't got nothing. If you are not getting revelation from God that tells that your relationship with and time spent with God is lacking. It also says that even if you covet and copy someone, you cannot do what they do if you don't have Love. The fact that you don't have revelation and relationship is saying that you don't have Love.

Jesus is stable and constant and is the same yesterday, today, and forever, we need that dependability, that stability in people, and especially in God, but doesn't everyone like a little variety in some things? Yes, even God. That is why the gifts are given as God wills and the administration is different according to how individuals do and share their ministry gifts with others. It is so the variety of people that God created will be reached by these different administrations of the gifts.

Sabotaging gifts happens in churches too often. Once is too often. The gift is given by God, for people, yet those who are jealous of people or of giftings would just as soon shut the gift down to shut the person down, or shut the person up. They don't care and haven't given a care to what God is doing in this person's life.

Better ask God, *Who is this person to you?* And then handle that person accordingly. If that person has nothing to do with you, then step away. God will move them if they need to be moved. I am speaking of lay person to lay person and I am speaking of people in leadership dealing with others in leadership as well as leadership-to-lay person dynamics. Touch not God's anointed.

Anyone who has ever been sat down in a church knows what I'm talking about. Anyone who has ever been unceremoniously removed from a position in a church knows what I'm talking about. Anyone who has been silenced in a church or by a church leader knows. Anyone who has ever experienced rejection for no apparent reason in a church— hey. It's for one of two reasons, or both: Your gift is great in the Lord and the person over you is threatened and realizes that they can't be over you. And/or for that reason you are not supposed to be there in that season, so God is moving you or preparing to move you. Still, there is no reason for the person or person in the place where you currently are not to show you Grace as they pray with you and for you that the Lord will lead you to your right place and position.

You don't have to try to hurt and hate someone to let them go. Well, unless you have rejection issues yourself.

As a co-pastor in a ministry, and by the Spirit of God I told my husband, the pastor that these three couples were fully developed and needed to be sent out to start their own churches. As he called himself Apostolic this was the perfect set up for him/us to help them plant new churches. I was shut down for mentioning such a thing. Within two years, two of those couples were split up and wandering church wise. The third couple is still at that church, and they appear dried up and unfulfilled, just going through the motions.

Those three couples--, that's six adults and their children too, because they suffered, were **sacrificed** on the pharaonic altar of *I don't want to let them go*. Or the altar of, *Their tithes are too good to let them go*. Or, if they go, won't they take people with them?

Saints of God: the prophetic identifies. It is what we do. Listen as God speaks through prophetic voices. He says He will not do anything unless He first reveals it to His prophets. Shutting the mouth of a prophet is very unwise if that prophet is speaking what *Thus saith the Lord.* So many want to only hear what they want to hear, saying, *Prophesy to us lightly.*

Lord, have Mercy!

What Altar Is This?

You can know if an altar is of God or if it is an evil altar by asking the Holy Spirit.

With your own eyes and discernment, you can evaluate the altar by its fruit. What is coming out of that place? What is emanating from that place? Whatever it is, it is because of the altar that is there.

Or, is there more than one altar in a place? Can there be more than one altar in a family?

Possibly.

There was a family of saved Christians, so that family would have a Godly altar, right?

An altar can be a physical thing, and/or an altar is a spiritual thing. If a family worships God, but they have no physical, tangible altar in the home, then their altar is spiritual.

But can one home, one family have more than one altar? Possibly and probably. Depending on what those people worship in that family. Is the family on one-accord, or does anything go? This goes back to leadership, does it not?

The last born in that Christian family decided to build an altar in her bedroom after all the other children had grown up, married, and left home. Her mother laughed, thinking it was funny to hear the teen chanting sounds at what she told her mother was a Buddhist altar.

The family began to fall apart, even the family members who were grown and gone. Marriages began to disintegrate. The grandchildren in that family started to go astray. There were house fires at three different houses. That particular house ended up burning down to the ground. It became known later that this was a witchcraft altar, not a Buddhist altar at all. Either way it was not of

God. Buddha was not God. But what seemed to happen is that the Christian altar wasn't being attended to as usual, but the other foreign altar was priested over by this evil and/or deceived teenager.

What is the strongest altar? What is the predominant altar? The one that is getting attention, worship, and sacrifices. The altar that gets the most attention, worship and the biggest sacrifices is the strongest altar at the time, although God is the greatest power, always.

In the same way, even at a church if the hateful new-people-hating, friend-faking, new single female disdaining altar is being serviced by many souls, or by the stronger souls in a church, for example, then it is the stronger altar.

Can You See Me?

I've heard countless stories of what I'm about to share, but it is safer to tell my own. I've been to many prophetic conferences and meetings but very few have ever called me up for a word. Even in a small setting where everyone else is getting a word, or ministry, or deliverance or something, but I'm getting nothing.

I would celebrate with those who received a prophetic word, but I have felt invisible for years. So, I made sure to seek God for myself and not solely depend on prophecy or the prayers of others.

Even when I left a marriage and therefore a ministry, as the co-pastor, I felt led of the Lord to start a home cell. I obeyed God, I got everything that God said to do to prepare, but no one covered me, or authorized, as they say--, released me to do ministry that God put in me. One person did reach out to me, but he was insincere and tried to hit on me. Therefore, no real, genuine "covering" would call me back. I was looking for spiritual covering, but I suppose that people don't do that anymore?

Yes, they do.

After some years, of myself wandering and practically giving up on ministry, I came back to my senses – Thank YOU, Lord, and let God, Himself release me and just stepped out.

I have always respected positions in a church, titles, and offices of course; but mostly I respect anointing. I will then suppose that those who do not have authority to prophesy to me do not attempt it. Many years ago, a man called me out in a small setting to prophesy to me and what he said, unless it is for some future time, had absolutely nothing to do with me. So, the answer is, no, many do not see me and/or are not called to prophesy to me. I'm okay with that.

Let us all be wise and not force prophecy, or force a *word*, or make up a word to tell anyone. It's how a lot of trouble will start. It can lead a person on the wrong path for their lives; it can jump them into a demonic timeline and out of the path of their destiny, altogether.

A forced prophetic word coming out of a prideful person is Church *Craft,* especially if the false prophet attempts to MAKE *their* word true to save face. Sometimes a face should not be saved; that face should be facing the person who received the erroneous "word," and apologizing and renouncing the error. Or, that face should be on the ground, on the floor, repenting. I know my forehead has been in the carpet of my house as I have repented to God for wrongs I have done. A minister of God cannot lack humility and a quickness to repent. God resists the prideful, but He runs to the humble.

As famous athletes do, you cannot SAY you are humble, that is bragging that you are humble. That is pride; it is fake humility. For a man to seek out his own glory is not glory at all. Someone else says you are humble, you don't and can't say it yourself. Humility is observed; it is not announced by the person. Think about it, that is seeking glory for being humble. *Huh?*

Ten Lies

When you catch someone in a lie you may have any number of reactions. When you catch someone in ten lies, what is your response then? Lying is such a big thing in our world that it has categories: there is compulsory lying, and pathological lies.

Pathological liars can be very manipulative and generally lie to get their way. They have little to no regard for whom they hurt. Their lies are usually very dramatic, complicated, and detailed. These folks are dangerous because they believe their own lies. I worked with a girl who had an amazing college major going on, drove a Mercedes truck, and was just months from graduating with a degree in cyber security. In a few weeks it was found out that she was not in school, lived at home with her mother, at age 27, and had no vehicle, but took an Uber for transportation.

The compulsive liar generally knows right from wrong, but chooses to lie, usually to get out of some other lie they've told previously.

Would *ten lies* come from a pathological or a compulsory liar? It depends.

In the natural, and in terms of a DSM diagnosis, pathological lying is a possible symptom of certain personality disorders, including borderline personality disorder, or narcissistic personality disorder, or antisocial personality disorder. A false prophet, for example, who will want to insist that their false *word* is true is a narcissist. Narcissists can never be wrong; the rest of the world, sure--, but never them. There is not an iota of humility in a narcissist. Further a prideful person will not be quick to repent; a narcissist will never repent. Their goal is to be right, prove they are right, and if necessary, prove everyone else wrong to assert their rightness. It starts with lies and can escalate to violence if that narcissist's huge ego feels threatened.

The *spiritual* cause of lying of any variety is the *spirit of lying*, *a lying spirit*, and or a strongman of lying. Deliverance is needed.

A single female in a church asked the choir director why the praise team aren't wearing the hats she got for them. The director didn't know.

I am that single female, so I asked the praise team members, and they said, *"We don't decide what we are going to wear, the choir director decides what we are going to wear and when."* Nothing seems to happen regarding these hats for months. So, I asked the choir director again and the director lied and, *again*, pretended she didn't know anything about what the choir wears.

I asked the music minister to make some background warfare prayer music for me, for which I would pay him. He never got around to doing it, but looked sheepishly at me every time I asked him about it – about once per month for about three months, then I realized he's never going to do this, although I've offered to pay him. Even though he claims he didn't want pay. I believe he's been told NOT to do it.

When the hats were presented as a gift to the choir, the single female was told, "*We are not looking for anyone older to be in the choir; we are only looking for young people.*" (OMG, as if I'd want to be associated with that "choir"). So, they got one new singer--, a young person, but they can't control how tight or suggestive her clothes are. They refuse to wear choir robes, but the choir director displays tantrums and mad attempts at control, which is witchcraft—Church *Craft*.

Mirror, mirror on the wall, who's the most insecure person of all? And why is this person trying to control everyone in the building, or block everything that I, myself am doing in a supposed-to-be house of God? Saints, when you see or sense something like that going on, you step back and just watch. And listen. Discern.

That Guy

Single females? You should have known that a guy was involved somehow---.

So, I asked about *that* guy who caught my attention in service because he came and sat by me Sunday after Sunday. The answer to my question was, *"That guy? I don't know anything about him just that he comes here with someone, so ask that woman about him."*

Two days later more information was "leaked" to me, without me ever bringing *That Guy* up: *"That guy? His ex-wife did a number* on him, ruined his career and took him for all he has, so he's broke."

I found out later that the man has never been married, so there is no ex-wife.

"That guy? Don't tell him that you like him! Definitely don't tell him that you like him."

Now, I wonder why not? So, I asked God who said it was fine for me to tell him. Therefore, I told him that I like him, and that is the thing he's most happy about. He even told me how happy he is that I told him that I like him.

"That guy? He's not coming to the deliverance retreat, and he hasn't signed up for it. So he's not coming." I heard a very pleased tone of voice over the phone as I was told that.

I spoke to *That Guy* two days later and he told me that he was attending the meetings. The irony is if I thought that guy was coming to the retreat I wouldn't have. But since I was told he was not coming, I felt I wouldn't be too embarrassed to be in a meeting like that, in his presence, all vulnerable, and *what not.*

"That guy? He probably doesn't know anything about fasting."

I talked to *That Guy,* and he knows more than you do about fasting and could probably teach it very well.

"That guy?" she's volunteering more information again. I didn't ask her anything, but this time she says, *"That guy? He's like a know-it-all."*

Time has gone by, and I've gotten to know *That Guy,* who, in my opinion is a very educated, confident, grown man who knows what he knows and has studied to show himself approved. But he is not arrogant.

"That guy? Maybe he was looking for somebody with money."

Yes, that was said to me. That line took the cake. That was a double slam. So, is this scheming or rambling talker saying the only quality about me that would cause a person to sit by me in church is that I **appear** to have money? Or is this prattler saying that *that guy* doesn't have any character and is a gold-digger? *Either* of those two statements is foul and demeaning.

I was told one more thing that I cannot bear to type or put into print; the Holy Spirit constrains me. But know that it was grievous. After so many **lies**, why would I believe anything else this person says?

Would you?

So, these lies, at least the ones involving *that guy*, were because a prophetic "word" had been given and it was error, all error and now the person who gave that so-called *word* has resorted to lying to try to force that *word* to be true.

It cannot be forced because I didn't believe any of the lies. It seemed that I, one single female was the threat to the fake prophetic word, I was the threat to the strategy an plans of one or more evil women. It seems this single female was the only threat to whatever they were planning, so they planned among other things to put a rock of offense in front of me to try to make me stumble.

Church *Craft*.

The lies only made me do the opposite of what they were designed to do. The lies made me look harder, listen closer, and seek God more, and seek to know what the motivation behind the lies was.

At the same time, I became very leery of the lies, as I do not tolerate lies very well. Or, I should say the Holy Spirit in me doesn't tolerate lies.

The real question is, how should *I* have been the gauge or the threat to the lies? Where is the Holy Spirit? The Holy Spirit convicts of sin. The Holy Spirit leads folks into all Truth.

The Holy Spirit is why my face is on the ground repenting to God when I am wrong, wrong, wrong. Why is it not the same for them?

I'm not the Holy Spirit. I'm a person.

The fear of God is lacking somewhere on several grounds. First, quenching, ignoring or grieving the Holy Spirit is not a consideration here--, lie after lie. Is there a seared conscience, or is someone all the way reprobate in their mind? How am *I* the threat to the first lie—the fake prophetic word. I wasn't even there--, the Holy Spirit has revealed this to me. Oh, come on people, we are all human and folks can make mistakes. But we apologize and repent and take back things that we say in error. God understands.

But to stay on that lie and try to enforce the lie as truth especially with more and more lies, that's another whole thing.

Why had the Holy Spirit been shut down? I say that because if the repentance was quick the other lies and attempts at deception would never have happened.

In the Gospel of Luke when Zaccheus was getting saved, he confessed to Jesus:

...and if I have taken anything from any man by false accusation, I restore him fourfold.
(Luke 19:8B)

I have shared the things said about *That Guy* to me. I have not shared what was said about me to *That Guy*. I'm not naïve enough to think that even while they smiled in my face nothing was said about me in attempts to keep us apart.

The irony is all the while this was going on, there was a series being taught from the pulpit about SOULS being bought and sold. Like a bad movie villain in a soliloquy telling what evil they are doing as they are doing it. Narrating their own plots to the audience.

Soul merchants in a church are actively practicing Church Craft. The purpose of buying or selling a soul is for sacrifice. *That Guy* was being bought to be sold to a "friend" or some woman as a **husband**.

The single female who they tried to defraud, or trick out of a divine connection was to be sold as a sacrifice so she wouldn't even *need* a divine connection.

But God said something like, **This will not be**, and revealed the whole plot in real time.

Christians do not sacrifice one another but witches and occultists do. This is straight up Church *Craft*.

Has this ever happened to you, or is it currently happening to you? If so, do you need to run right now? And, I don't mean *around* that sanctuary, but **out** of it???

Enough Is Enough?

Folks love to say, enough is enough, but really, how much is *enough*? If I were a vindictive soul I'd be asking God, "*How could You let that person tell me so many lies and be so manipulative, and putting up obstacles for me while trying to be my fake friend?"* But I'm not that person.

God's got this.

The Word says that God will not ever put more on you than you can bear. But the devil, he will load you, overload you, overwhelm you – he doesn't care.

We pray and ask God for resolutions to problems, but it when God says it is enough--, it is enough.

> And he said unto Abram, Know of a surety that thy seed shall be a stranger in a land [that is] not theirs, and shall serve them; and they shall afflict them four hundred years; And also that nation, whom they shall serve, will I judge: and afterward shall they come out with great substance. And thou shalt go to thy fathers in peace; thou shalt be buried in a good old age. But in the fourth generation they shall come hither again: **for the iniquity of the Amorites [is] not yet full**.
> (Genesis 15:14-16)

I was as a stranger in that place. I was afflicted, even while trying to serve there.

That's why I say the Lord has got this; He will judge. And, I expect to come out with great spoils for standing for what is right because God will avenge all disobedience in my obedience; thank You, Lord.

The command of God to take the land from the Canaanite peoples (Deut. 20) would come only when their iniquity was complete. The Amorites were piling sin upon sin, but their sin was not yet full, therefore God wasn't judging it yet.

Do you take the trash out before it is full? Sometimes, *right*? It depends on what's in it—is it stinking up to high Heaven, or about to smell up the place?   When someone is habitually sinning against you, you can call *time*. You can call Judgment, but it is when God says and sees that they've done quite enough and will never repent that He will send judgment to a person, a people, a land, a nation.

This is why it seems that people are still getting away with stuff--, even lie after lie.

In a church?

So much depends on the altar of that church. If it is a Godly altar, blatant sins will not be allowed or even expected. If some other entity is being worshipped there strongly, regularly, then what that idol *god*, who is not Jehovah allows is what will stand--, until the Sovereign God says otherwise.

Yes, your prayers are heard, and God will answer you, either suddenly, or in time. God is gracious and gives us Grace and time to repent, so He would do that for others as well. Even if you are inflamed with anger--, don't be, sinners sin against God. You may feel that they are sinning against you, but since you're not perfect, and I'm not perfect how can a sinner sin against another sinner? Well, it could happen, but who are you going to tell?

Lord, have Mercy on us all.

In His Grace, God gives us all time and space to repent of sins we commit.

Only if the Lord says so, withdraw your foot from that place, unless you like being lied to over and over. If God has you there to be lied to so that the iniquity the person is building up will become full, then stay there. If God says that 10 lies is enough for you to hear, you can leave now--, then leave.

Plead the Blood of Jesus over all worship you have done in that place regarding any ungodliness being sponsored by the altar in that place. Plead the Blood if you've been led to make ungodly, soulish, or fleshly prayers, decrees, or declarations in that place. Repent of serving an evil altar if that has been the case where you are. Again, know them by their fruit, and the Holy Spirit will lead you to all Truth.

Pray. Pray for Mercy and forgiveness. If you are praying judgment, make sure you are sure and you are clear about such a thing, it is very serious. If you hear the Lord declaring judgment, if He has revealed that to you, then that is another whole thing.

Clear! Clear! Clear! Stand clear if you know that a people or a place, a nation, or a land are under judgment from God. Withdraw your foot from that place.

Being under judgment from God is serious; falling into the hands of an angry God--, is anybody else afraid of God?

Idols rage and rampage all the time, stealing, killing, and destroying when they, (both idol *gods*, and people who believe themselves to be idols) that are used to being worshipped, are no longer being worshipped. They, through the Accuser of the Brethren, go to the Throne of God with evil petitions to get judgments against mankind to get permission to do evil to people.

They can hold their own courts, witchcraft courts, occultic courts and the various evil Councils that run this world can all come up with their own evil verdicts and sentences. Two or more may come together for their own evil purposes, even against *you*. This is another reason to always stay prayerful.

Behold, they shall surely gather together, but
not by me: whosoever shall gather together
against thee shall fall for thy sake.
(Isaiah 54:15)

In the Courts of Heaven they will show their documents, their evil covenants that some ancestor, or you, yourself agreed to, to prove that you OWE them. They will then desire that God declare you guilty.

If you are not even in the Courts of Heaven when this is happening, you lose. If you have no counter to this Evil Petition, you lose. Don't forget Satan is doing this 24/7. How many times a day do you sin? That's how many times he's probably up there accusing you, every day. How many times a day do you pray? In Wisdom and obedience, it would be best to be praying and repenting every time you sin. Defensively, it would be wise to be praying at least as many times as Satan is up in Heaven accusing you to God. Offensively, wouldn't it be better to be praying _instead_ of sinning so that Satan has nothing on you to even go to the Courts of Heaven to accuse you about?

Best to repent quickly when you sin. And, you become aware that you sinned, how? The Holy Spirit will bring you under conviction. TURN ON your Holy Spirit

Notifications; do not turn them off. Do not ignore, quench, or grieve the Holy Spirit.

In the Courts of Heaven, you can always win if you show up--, if you allow Jesus to be your Advocate, as He is. If you admit to your guilt; you are guilty, all of us are, you still can win. We have all sinned and fallen short of the Glory of God. Also to win, be aware that the Blood of Jesus is your Defense, and plead the Blood of Jesus.

Conversion Can Take A While

Church is a brazen place to do this Church *Craft*. Any form of witchcraft is totally against God, and His Doctrine. But, guards are down and who with a pure heart would ever suspect such a thing in a church?

Well..., at first, we may not, but eventually we all will see patterns, motives, and catch the ill-treatment and lies. This all boils down to spiritual abuse because that is not what any of us go to a church for--, or expecting.

Blindly a person could be practicing Church *Craft* because they are really not saved, but believe they are.

Or, the person may be saved, that is really between them and God, but their soul has not been converted. They know how to *act* in front of folks, but they aren't really what they are acting like. Everyone in a church is not a Christian. There can be a dark, occultic or witchcraft side to some, even those who have positions, even in a church. Folks, we have to always discern *spirits*.

Conversion can take a while; it can take a lifetime if one is prideful, insisting on tradition, and not listening to the Holy Spirit. When a person believes their own spirit is already holy, why would they listen to God's Spirit? All the ways of a man are clean in his own eyes—that means that that man believes that he is right, he may be the only one who is right, he is smart, possibly--, probably the smartest person in the world; therefore, *he* is holy. He thinks like a Pharisee, why would he need advice from anyone?

The law of the LORD is perfect, converting the soul: (Psalm 19:7)

When a man with years of military experience retired from Service, he then went on to get a seminary degree where he intensely studied the Word. Shouldn't he be converted by now? Instead, he is a holy terror right now. In his own mind, he is not wrong, he is never wrong, everyone must listen to and obey him. So, he thinks.

God is running this, people; don't think you are. Studying the Word for exams only, as in school is not getting the Word in you. The

Word will convert the soul when applied. The Word of God is not just for others, it is for me and for you. The Word will change you, and that for **good**.

Once a pastor asked that anyone who felt that they had *arrived* to raise their hand. One lone lady raised her hand. She really believed she had *arrived*. I'm not sure how. She may have had a nice job, a nice car, a nice home, nice clothes--, but *arrived*? She was showing that she is willful and unteachable. Once you *arrive* don't you get off the train?

As it turned out, she was at that church with another woman's husband as her "man." How do I know? The man's wife came in during a prophetic conference to confront the man and drop off his twin teenaged boys to their dad. When that man's real wife *arrived*, it was ugly.

Are you ready for some irony? This cheating woman and cheating man came into that church together as a "couple," so they were well-received, even celebrated by all. Soon they were both in prominent positions and ministries within that church. Even after the real wife run-in, they maintained their ministry positions.

Go figure.

(But didn't I tell you that the single woman who wanted another woman's man already had him, and don't worry about yours?)

Folks who believe they have *arrived* are usually running things, or believe they are. They are the HNIC and that was their goal all along.

Yes, conversion can take a while, even if the person wants to be converted. If they don't want to be converted, it will never happen.

What Does God Say About That?

A minister is a servant, not a king. Ministers, especially, must be **good** to people.

Knowing how to talk sweet or baby talk when you want something, and snapping and going off on people when they are not "obeying" you is not leadership. That is knowing how to have a tantrum and attempting to rule with an iron fist. In the world's diagnosis it smacks of bipolarity. In spiritual terms, that is manipulation, domination, and control. Weren't all the evil kings in the Bible like that? That is witchcraft and when done in a church, that is Church *Craft.*

Satan wouldn't conform to what God, his creator made him for. God is merciful – Satan is still alive. A righteous king or leader must show Mercy. A leader with power must show Grace and Mercy and spend time in the presence of God to make sure they are not reigning in terror and also in error.

When a witch is angry that you won't do what they begin to act as if they are God, that they created *you,* and have the right to judge you and sentence and execute you. They show not one iota of Mercy because it is not in them, unless Christ is in them. But, when this type of hysterics and drama escalates into Church *Craft--,* that is, witchcraft within the church, the puppet master is believing that they are God and that they made you and all the other *puppets* on the pews.

I personally have heard more than my share of folk recounting, "what they've done for me." Of course, that means they thought you were **nothing** until you met them, and without them, you will go back to being nothing. This is a seriously egotistical statement.

One employee was disgruntled for being fired because she came in disgruntled, stayed angry, like daily, and wanted to poison the morale of the office. After being fired, she complained loudly as she went out the door about all she had done for this particular business. She had worked their two weeks and had never done anything that wasn't in her job description or that she hadn't been paid for.

But in her mind, she had "made" the business that had been in business for 20 or 30 years before she ever got there.

Where do these people come from?

A husband, having a fight with his wife after 6 weeks of marriage exclaimed, *After all these years, and after all I have done for you!* This couple had a whirlwind courtship where the man just couldn't wait to marry the woman.

The wife glared at him and said, *We've been knowing each other for six months, not years. And, what have you done for me?* It was then that she realized this man was standing there looking at her but having a flash-back fight with his first wife and this must be how he or they used to fight--, dirty. No wonder that marriage broke up. So, if this man doesn't learn how to communicate and resolve issues, even in an argument, the second marriage is going the route of the first.

It is then that she learned that closing the marriage deal in a few months was so the woman wouldn't discover that this is one of the things wrong with her new hubby. He had convinced her that the first wife was the whole problem. Saints of God when you meet a person like that who is taking zero responsibility for the breakup of his last relationship--, RUN!

Do not get together with a person who has no responsibility in the breakup of his last relationship and who has done no forensics to even see why it was broken up. Do not get together with the victim, the sole victim of a previous marriage or relationship or situationship. Chances are very good that the information you've been fed is either not true, inaccurate, skewed, or all three.

Women, we are too generous letting men go from relationship to relationship without any accountability. We can't let our own pride and ego make us believe we are so great that we will change him or that he will change because of our wonderfulness and be different. We can't believe that we will be *better* than the previous person he was with because **there may not have been anything wrong with *her*.**

Yes, there could have been something wrong with them *together*, but he has to as an adult, bear some of the responsibility as to why the marriage didn't work or broke up.

However, that doesn't mean that you can't have an accelerated courtship and marriage, it means that God has to be in it, full force. God has to be the one to put you two together. Else, you may be together, that is associated, but not put together, as in made one. Amen.

Tell Me More

Oh, you want to know more about those ten lies and why they were told. Let's look at the last seven lies since they were all about one person as an attempt to keep this writer from talking to that person. Yes, even while in the church, talking to a brother in the faith.

Conversion can take a while--, even in me. Therefore, if I've come to distrust you, and you tell me not to do something, unless God says the same, I'm likely to do the opposite. Especially when I check with God and God is telling me to do the opposite of what Church *Craft* is directing me to do; I will obey God.

But in terms of more, the light was really shined on the behavior of the owner of the ten lies when they were called out by another congregant who summed things up nicely by saying, *Since I've been here, I haven't felt the love, any love as I thought should be in a church.* She said much more than that and without malice or venom. She spoke steadily and with composure and love. I believed her. My spirit man bore witness that she was speaking truth, even to power. The Holy Spirit bore witness that she was telling the truth.

The moment of that girl's honesty and pain was very telling for me. I realized that what I was experiencing there was **fake**; if they can't love all, do they love *any*? The Holy Spirit let me know right then that if they have turned on this girl, and if they say they love me today, ***when* will they turn on me**?

That revelation soured in my spirit and my stomach, as if I had eaten the little book from the Bible that tasted good but was bitter in the belly. Oh, being treated as the darling coming in is sweet, but this new treatment was not sweet. Folks turn on each other for any of the reasons mentioned in this book and for many other reasons that have not, and may not be mentioned here.

FYI: I have learned the ___when___ of that previous question.

You have your own story, *don't you?*

Pay Attention, Or Pay

When I was not discerning, trekking into a place called *church*, I used to think they cared about me in that place, but now I see. Amazing Grace; thank You, Lord.

Oh, I didn't answer the *That Guy* question from the last chapter, did I?

Let me do that now.

At first, I thought there must really be something wrong with *That Guy* that this one person, in authority, lied on so easily and that is why they don't want me around him. Then, in a passive-aggressive way I saw and heard a male figure, also in a position of authority slamming *That Guy* from the pulpit, but at the same time they want to be around him; this does not add up. So, they don't want me around him, and they don't want him around me., What's wrong with either of us, except the stuff that is wrong with people who come to a church, which is why they come to the church?

What's wrong with that fellow? So, I asked him. He had no answer but I'm sure the fact that I asked him carried some weight. I also believe the Lord will speak to him.

I also asked God, Lord, what is wrong with *me*?

This place was now giving high school clique vibes. Of note, I ran the cliques at my high school, so not being in one, when I am one of the cool people was not cool. But it really was the feeling of knowing there is a secret club was suspect, since God is not about that. God is of the Light, not of the darkness. Therefore, I got to stepping, especially when the soulish and demonic prayers started against me and my physical person and safety.

Oh, what happened? That's what she wanted to know from me. She asked me, *Oh, what happened?* She was trying to find out if their evil prayers were hitting or not. Within the warfare, I cannot say, but if you are a reader of my books, you know that I will end up telling you, but later, once the warfare has ended.

Take that counsel for yourself as well. Sometimes your mouth has to remain shut to not give away your status and your position to the enemy in the heat of battle, especially spiritual battles.

Church *Craft* creates enemies because the person or persons doing the craft have already declared you an enemy, although you are not and never went there as an enemy, not even from Day One. Saints of God, if someone makes you an enemy, then they are now involved in the process of you becoming a soldier, a warrior. Fight for your life, don't just sit there and take assault, injury and evil arrows.

Yes, God will teach your hands to fight and if He is using self-proclaimed Amorites who rise up to fight you, even for no real reason, then so be it. Let God be God.

Thou hast thrust sore at me that I might fall:
but the LORD helped me. (Psalm 118:13)

Is This A Strange Altar?

It's as though they wanted to worship *That Guy*, or really, any of the guys that I have mentioned in this book as commodities or fish, while their women, or the single woman is the bones of that fish. Is this man a strange altar? What is going on here?

They wanted to get rid of me, and worship him. What? *Why?*

If they want to get rid of one and worship the other, then **the one they want to get rid of is the <u>sacrifice</u>.** Do you see how demonic Church *Craft* is?

Oh, readers, I can't surprise you. What is the end game of this worship? Is it money? Or is it to acquire some other item that will bring notoriety, prestige, or fame? Is it all four? Is it the hope for all four? If a person or people of a certain greed level roll up on someone that they think has money, they will try to sequester that person for themselves, especially if they think that person will give them money. If they meet a person who has something else that they value and covet and think they are smarter than the person who has that something and can dupe or bilk him out of it, they may set their evil plans in motion. Well, there you go, typical strongman behavior.

This is also how fake caregivers treat older people that they are supposed to take care of late in life, yet that caregiver blocks others from visiting this sunsetting or transitioning soul and ends up with all or most of the old or dying person's property.

None of this is sensical either because we are supposed to get our blessings and benefits from Jesus, not spying out the property of other people and then going for those items, like vultures awaiting death of the rightful owner.

Let's keep it real: if someone will sacrifice one, why wouldn't they sacrifice another? That is what I learned from the other young lady who *felt no love* in the place.

I saw three souls trying to be handled by would-be soul merchants. The first was the young lady that was so church hurt.

I was the second, and *That Guy* was the third. In which order, I do not know. But of me and *That Guy*, we were both on auction blocks to be sold, He was *to be* the husband of the lady who received the fake prophecy from *Potiphar's wife*.

They didn't care where the single female was sold to--, could have been Egypt for all they cared; they just wanted her gone. **But God said, NO! God said NO to both of those plans. Thank You, Lord.**

Love cannot be faked--, not real love. Love also doesn't just stop one day and become hate. There was never any love in that place.

Many waters cannot quench love, neither can the floods drown it: (Song 8:7A)

In discovering that there is no Love in there the real <u>altar</u> is revealed. Now we see *That Guy* may not have been set up as a strange altar, because he was also on a soul auction block. People do not sell their idols.

As heinous as selling a soul is, it is done out of the lust of money or some other gain. Selling souls is occultic, it is witchcraft as well as exchanging money in the House of God. My Bible says that Jesus turned over the tables of the money changers. Soul merchants are money changers.

The altar in that place is **Mammon** and the temptations are such as the baubles of Jesus' wilderness temptations. Why is a church a wilderness? You tell me. Who invited Satan? You tell me. Why don't these people either know better, or resist harder? Because they don't want to.

Does *That Guy* have money? Will he give them money or something else of value that they've spied out? I know the answer, but we are still in warfare, so I can't say just yet. But God knows; and God has the final word.

In the sense that the woman's desire shall be toward the man which is under the Curse of the Law from Genesis, single females are ejected, rejected, or even given over as candidates to be sacrificed in some places *called* churches by those churches. It seems that is so the man can be kept, worshipped, or used. But when you are messing with the life and the destiny of another person to please yourself or make yourself look good, that's self-worship while attempting to sacrifice another human being.

The *desire* of the woman is to rule **over** the man; is the Church trying to collect men and discard women? It shouldn't be, but if it is, that is Church *Craft* in one of its ugliest forms.

Spoils

Blessed are ye, when men shall revile you,
and persecute you, and shall say all manner
of evil against you falsely, for my sake.
Rejoice, and be exceeding glad: for great is
your reward in heaven: for so persecuted
they the prophets which were before you.
(Matthew 5:11-13)

If you are in a situation or place where
you are being reviled or persecuted and God

sent you there, stay there. Remain until God says to leave. If you are being persecuted for the sake of the Gospel, then you shall receive 100-fold return in this lifetime for that persecution.

If God says stay, then do what He says.

When God says, *Leave*, do that. It could be because of your gifting, anointing, purpose, and destiny that you are being despised in a place and it is time to break camp. Do what the Lord says. Saints now you see why it is so important for you to be able to hear from God for yourself. Amen.

There may be times you submit to authority even while seeing and enduring Church *Craft*. There may be times that you don't, and you must shake the dust. God knows. Ask Him and He will always answer. But know that what you do for the Lord, what you do for the Kingdom, He will in no wise cast you out, and He will reward those who believe that He is and diligently seek Him.

But it is good for me to draw near to God: I have put my trust in the Lord GOD, that I may declare all thy works. (Psalm 73:28)

AMEN.

Dear Reader

Thank you for acquiring, reading, and sharing this book. I hope that it will speak to you where you are if you've ever been rejected by a church or the alleged saved people in it.

Do not let them deter you from what God has called you to do. Listen for God's voice and do what He says, and it all will be well with you.

Pray for those who despitefully use you and God will avenge all disobedience in your obedience.

In the Name of Jesus,

Amen.

Dr. Marlene Miles

Prayer books by this author

While most books by this author have prayer points either throughout the book or at the end, there are some books that are **only** prayers. You just open up the book and pray. They are listed below:

Prayers Against Barrenness: *For Success in Business and Life*

Fruit of the Womb: *Prayers Against Barrenness*

Beauty Curses, *Warfare Prayers Against* https://a.co/d/5Xlc20M

Courts of Marriage: Prayers for Marriage in the Courts of Heaven *(prayerbook)*
https://a.co/d/cNAdgAq

Courtroom Warfare @ Midnight *(prayerbook)*
https://a.co/d/5fc7Qdp

Demonic Cobwebs *(prayerbook)* https://a.co/d/fp9Oa2H

Every Evil Bird https://a.co/d/hF1kh1O

Every Evil Arrow https://a.co/d/afgRkiA

Gates of Thanksgiving

Spirits of Death & the Grave, Pass Over Me and My House https://a.co/d/dS4ewyr

*Please note that my name is spelled incorrectly on amazon, but not on the book.

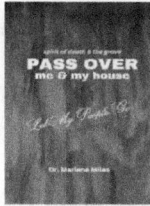

Throne of Grace: Courtroom Prayer

https://a.co/d/fNMxcM9

Warfare Prayer Against Poverty

https://a.co/d/bZ61lYu

Other books by this author

AK: *The Adventures of the Agape Kid*

AMONG SOME THIEVES

Ancestral Powers https://a.co/d/9prTyFf

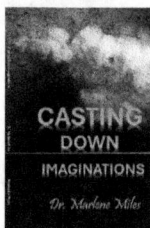

The Devourers: Thieves of Darkness 2

Do Not Swear by the Moon

Don't Refuse Me, Lord (4 book series)
https://a.co/d/idP34LG

Dream Defilement

The Emptiers: *Thieves of Darkness, 1*
https://a.co/d/5I4n5mc

Every Evil Arrow https://a.co/d/afgRkiA

Evil Touch https://a.co/d/gSGGpS1

Failed Assignment https://a.co/d/3CXtjZY

Fantasy Spirit Spouse https://a.co/d/hW7oYbX

FAT Demons (The): *Breaking Demonic Curses*

The Fold (5-book series)

- The Fold (Book 1)
- Name Your Seed (Book 2)
- The Poor Attitudes of Money (3)
- Do Not Orphan Your Seed (4)
- For the Sake of the Gospel (5)
- My Sowing Journal

Gang Ups: Touch Not God's Anointed

got HEALING? Verses for Life

got LOVE? Verses for Life

got HOPE? Verses for Life

got money? https://a.co/d/g2av41N

How to Dental Assist

How to Dental Assist2: Be Productive, Not Wasteful

I Take It Back

Legacy

Let Me Have A Dollar's Worth https://a.co/d/h8F8XgE

Level the Playing Field

Living for the NOW of God

Lose My Location https://a.co/d/crD6mV9

Man Safari, *The*

Marriage Ed. Rules of Engagement & Marriage

Made Perfect in Love

Money Hunters: Beware of Those

Money on the Altar https://a.co/d/4EqJ2Nr

Mulberry Tree https://a.co/d/9nR9rRb

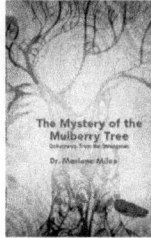

Motherboard (The) - *Soul Prosperity Series*

Name Your Seed

Occupy: *Until I Return*

Plantation Souls

Players Gonna Play

Power Money: Nine Times the Tithe
https://a.co/d/gRt41gy

The Power of Wealth *(forthcoming)*

Powers Above

Repent of Visiting Evil Altars
https://a.co/d/3n3Zjwx

The Robe, Part 1, The Lessons of Joseph

The Robe, Part II, The Lessons of Joseph

Seasons of Grief

Seasons of Waiting

Seasons of War

Second Marriage, Third--, *Any Marriage*

https://a.co/d/6m6GN4N

Sift You Like Wheat

Six Men Short: What Has Happened to all the Men?

Soul Prosperity soul prosperity series 3

https://a.co/d/5p8YvCN

Souls Captivity soul prosperity series 2

The Spirit of Poverty

StarStruck

SUNBLOCK

The Swallowers: *Thieves of Darkness,* 3

Take It Back

This Is NOT That: How to Keep Demons from Coming at You

Time Is of the Essence

Too Many Wives: *Why You Have Lady Problems*

Tormenting Spirits   https://a.co/d/dAogEJf

Toxic Souls

Triangular Power *(series)*

- Powers Above
- SUNBLOCK

- Do Not Swear by the Moon
- STARSTRUCK

Uncontested Doom

Unguarded Hours, *The*

Unseen Life, *The* https://a.co/d/0drZ5Ll

Upgrade: How to Get Out of Survival Mode

- Toxic Souls (Book 2 of series)
- Legacy (Book 3 of series)

The Wasters: *Thieves of Darkness,* Bk 2
https://a.co/d/bUvI9Jo

What Have You to Declare? What Do You Have With You from Where You've Been?

When I Was A Child, *I Prayed As a Child*

When the Devourer is Rebuked

https://a.co/d/1HVv8oq

The Wilderness Romance *(series)* This series is about conducting a Godly relationship and marriage with someone who is a Wilderness person. It is about how to recognize it and navigate through it. These books are about how not to get caught up in such.

- *The Social Wilderness*
- *The Sexual Wilderness*
- *The Spiritual Wilderness*

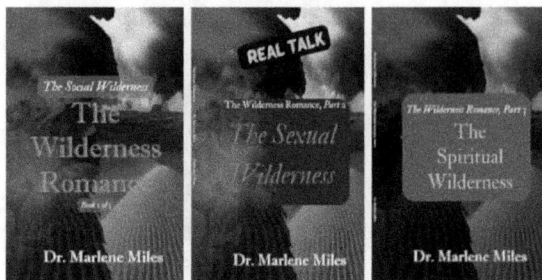

Other Series

The Fold (a series on Godly finances)
https://a.co/d/4hz3unj

Soul Prosperity Series https://a.co/d/bz2M42q

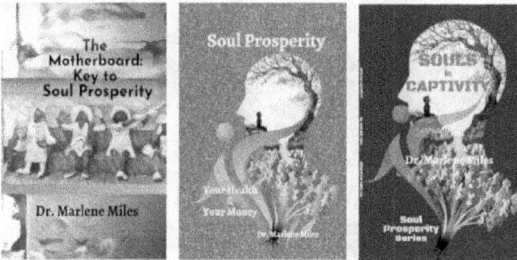

Spirit Spouse books

https://a.co/d/9VehDSo https://a.co/d/97sKOwm

Thieves of Darkness series

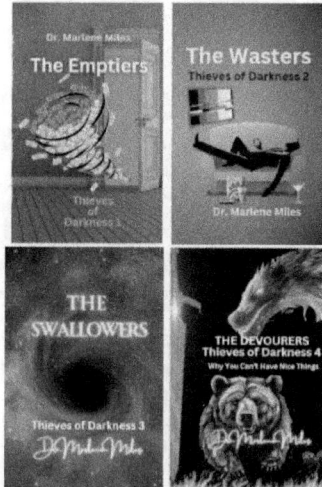

Triangular Powers https://a.co/d/aUCjAWC

Upgrade (series) *How to Get Out of Survival Mode*
https://a.co/d/aTERhX0